SUNSET HOTEL, BARNEGAT LIGHT — *Originally called the Sans Souci, the Sunset Hotel, at left, on the bay side of Barnegat Inlet, attracted sportsmen to the isolated northern end of Long Beach Island. Built in 1883, it burned to the ground in a spectacular blaze in June 1932. This late 1800s photograph is from the book* Six Miles At Sea.

A Cormorant Card
© Down The Shore Publishing, Box 3100, Harvey Cedars, NJ 08008

BARNEGAT LIGHTHOUSE — *This turn of the century view of the lighthouse shows the magnificent keeper's house built in 1889 and sold for scrap in 1920 after severe coastal erosion threatened the twenty-room structure. A lighthouse was first built here in 1834, and this is the second and present-day lighthouse, completed in 1859. From the book* Six Miles At Sea.

A Cormorant Card
© Down The Shore Publishing, Box 3100, Harvey Cedars, NJ 08008

WHARF, DOCK ROAD, BEACH HAVEN — *The steamboat wharf at the end of Dock Road in Beach Haven was a gathering spot on summer afternoons in the late 1800s. Before the coming of the railroad and a causeway, this was where most people arrived on Long Beach Island. Photograph by Robert F. Engle, from the book* Eighteen Miles of History on Long Beach Island.

CATBOATS, LITTLE EGG HARBOR BAY — *The traditional Barnegat Bay catboat was used for transportation to and from Long Beach Island, for fishing charters, as a mail boat, and for recreational racing. This turn-of-the-century view, in the bay off of Beach Haven, is from the book* Six Miles At Sea.

A Cormorant Card
© Down The Shore Publishing, Box 3100, Harvey Cedars, NJ 08008

OCEAN BATHING, BEACH HAVEN — *After the long train journey from Philadelphia, early summer visitors to Beach Haven would stroll the boardwalk and take a dip in the Atlantic before dinner at the resort's grand hotels, such as the Engleside, shown here, with its distinctive conical tower. This photograph, by Earl C. Roper, circa 1920, is from the book* Six Miles At Sea.

A Cormorant Card
© Down The Shore Publishing, Box 3100, Harvey Cedars, NJ 08008

ENGLESIDE HOTEL GUESTS, BEACH HAVEN — *The Engles, father and son hoteliers, regularly organized activities and events for their guests. In this photograph, circa 1903, guests clown on the beach for Robert F. Engle, the son, a serious photographer whose glass negatives have preserved much of turn-of-the-century Beach Haven. From the book* Eighteen Miles of History.

A Cormorant Card
© Down The Shore Publishing, Box 3100, Harvey Cedars, NJ 08008

DOCK ROAD, BEACH HAVEN — *Catboats hoist sail near the first Beach Haven Yacht Club in 1883. Summer visitors, workers, and residents would all arrive at this dirt road to the bay by sailboat or steamboat from the mainland until a railroad bridge was built to Long Beach Island in 1886. From the book* Eighteen Miles of History.

A Cormorant Card
© Down The Shore Publishing, Box 3100, Harvey Cedars, NJ 08008

BEACH HAVEN YACHT CLUB DOCKS — *Catboats and row-boats tie up at the yacht club dock in this photograph by Robert F. Engle, circa 1900. The legendary Acme Hotel is in the distance to the left of the dock. From the book* Eighteen Miles of History.

A Cormorant Card
© Down The Shore Publishing, Box 3100, Harvey Cedars, NJ 08008

MANAHAWKIN AND LONG BEACH RAILROAD — *A train passes through a stretch of Harvey Cedars. Owned by the Pennsylvania Railroad, and operated by the Tuckerton Railroad, trains ran on Long Beach Island from 1886 until a nor'easter destroyed the trestle over Manahawkin Bay in 1935. From the book* Six Miles at Sea.

A Cormorant Card
© Down The Shore Publishing, Box 3100, Harvey Cedars, NJ 08008

TRAIN STOP, BEACH HAVEN TERRACE — *Although the Pennsylvania Railroad built only two stations on Long Beach Island (in Barnegat Light and Beach Haven) small communities such as Beach Haven Terrace built thier own in the early 1900s to spur development in vast desolate stretches of bogs, bayberry, and sand dunes. From the book* Eighteen Miles of History.

THE BOARDWALK, BEACH HAVEN — *In 1912, some of the resort's fashionable hotel guests stroll the town's earliest boardwalk with a porter from the Engleside Hotel. Modern acetylene gas lamps, installed in 1907, lit the walkway at night. The last boardwalk was destroyed in the hurricane of 1944 and never rebuilt. From the book* Eighteen Miles of History.

A Cormorant Card
© Down The Shore Publishing, Box 3100, Harvey Cedars, NJ 08008

DRIVING "DOWN THE SHORE" — *A real estate brochure promoted the joy and excitment of driving to the shore with the opening of the first automobile causeway to Long Beach Island in 1914. From the book* Six Miles at Sea.

A Cormorant Card
© Down The Shore Publishing, Box 3100, Harvey Cedars, NJ 08008

EDWARDIAN BEACH HAVEN — *Wooden ramps led from the boardwalk to the beach in 1905. Black was the color of choice for beachwear and umbrellas. From the book* Six Miles at Sea.

A Cormorant Card
© Down The Shore Publishing, Box 3100, Harvey Cedars, NJ 08008

HOTEL BALDWIN, BEACH HAVEN — *Minarets added gracefulness to the overwhelming size of the Hotel Baldwin, which stood between Pearl and Marine Streets from 1883 until 1960. The hotel burned in a spectacular night fire that could be seen from Toms River to Atlantic City. From the book* Six Miles at Sea.

A Cormorant Card
© Down The Shore Publishing, Box 3100, Harvey Cedars, NJ 08008

ON THE BEACH, BEACH HAVEN — *Timeless summertime pleasures, as seen in the mid-1930s, near the boardwalk and Engleside Hotel. From the book* Eighteen Miles of History.

A Cormorant Card
© Down The Shore Publishing, Box 3100, Harvey Cedars, NJ 08008

FISHING PIER, BEACH HAVEN — *Built out into the ocean from the boardwalk at Berkeley Avenue in 1924, the municipal fishing pier was popular with anglers until the 1944 Hurricane washed it away. From the book* Eighteen Miles of History.

A Cormorant Card
© Down The Shore Publishing, Box 3100, Harvey Cedars, NJ 08008

POUND FISHING — *The pound fishing industry began on Long Beach Island after the arrival of the railroad in 1886, was dominated by Scandanavians and Norwegians, and reached its peak in the 1930s with five major fisheries. The 1944 hurricane devastated the nets and poles and dwindling fish populations put an end to the last pound fishery, the Crest Fishery, in 1956. Photograph by Bill Kane from the book* Eighteen Miles of History.

A Cormorant Card
© Down The Shore Publishing, Box 3100, Harvey Cedars, NJ 08008

U.S. LIFESAVING SERVICE — *Captain John Marshall, with beard, poses with his crew at Bond's Life Saving Station at Holgate in 1888. The rugged lifesaving crews patrolled desolate beaches during the winter storm season from 1872 until 1915, when the service became the Coast Guard. From the book* Six Miles at Sea.

A Cormorant Card
© Down The Shore Publishing, Box 3100, Harvey Cedars, NJ 08008

WRECK OF THE *FORTUNA* — *The bark* Fortuna *washed ashore at Ship Bottom during a thick fog in January 1910, but it was a another wreck in the spring of 1817 that gave this town its unique name. From the book* Six Miles at Sea.

A Cormorant Card
© Down The Shore Publishing, Box 3100, Harvey Cedars, NJ 08008

THOMAS BOND — *Genial host of the legendary Long Beach House from 1851 to 1883 at what is now Holgate, Captain Bond was also the dedicated master of the U.S. Lifesaving station there. It was from the Long Beach House, and its influential guests, that came the genesis of Beach Haven in 1874. From the book* Eighteen Miles of History.... *Bond had a favorite poem, which he quoted often:*

A Name in the Sand
by Hannah Flagg Gould

Alone I walked the ocean strand
A pearly shell was in my hand
I stopped and wrote upon the sand
My name, the year, the date.

As onward from the spot I passed
One lingering look behind I cast
A wave came rolling high and fast
And washed my name away.

So shall it be, with every trace on earth of me.
A wave from dark oblivion's sea
Will roll across the place where I have trod
And leave no track or trace.

A Cormorant Card
© Down The Shore Publishing, Box 3100, Harvey Cedars, NJ 08008

CRABBING ON THE BAY — *Beach Haven, circa 1900. From the book* Six Miles at Sea.

A Cormorant Card
© Down The Shore Publishing, Box 3100, Harvey Cedars, NJ 08008

BARNEGAT LIGHT AND INLET — *Seen from the roof of the Sunset Hotel, circa 1900. Within twenty years, erosion would wash away all the dunes and tree-covered acreage to the left of the lighthouse, and the encroaching tides would prompt the government to sell the keeper's house for scrap. From the book* Six Miles at Sea.

A Cormorant Card
© Down The Shore Publishing, Box 3100, Harvey Cedars, NJ 08008